Tryst

A play

Colin Crowther

Samuel French—London
New York-Toronto-Hollywood

ISBN 0 573 12311 X

NL00018982

Please see page iv for further copyright information.

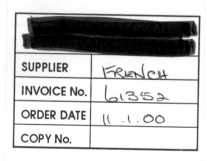

SUPPLIER	FRENCH
INVOICE No.	61352
ORDER DATE	11 . 1 . 00
COPY No.	

CHARACTERS

Jan, an artist, any age
Tom, 40–60
Brenda, his wife, 40–60

Note: The part of Jan could be played by a man, in which case
the pronunciation should be *Yan* and the lines at the end altered
accordingly.

The action of the play takes place in an art gallery, a living-
room, an art classroom, a studio, a hospital room and a room
in a vicarage.

Time — the present

COPYRIGHT INFORMATION
(See also page ii)

AUTHOR'S NOTE

Wardrobe

Modern, quiet, nothing distracting. Tom changes from overcoat to jacket to cardigan to dressing gown, but always over what he is already wearing. Brenda wears an overcoat over her dress, removing it at home. At one point she wears an apron over this. At another point she pulls Tom's cardigan over her shoulders. Jan wears a blouse and slacks. She dons a smock or similar painting coat, but only when she is actually working. She never leaves the stage, so this must hang, with an outdoor coat, over the upstage edge of the easel. The other two can leave the stage, occasionally, to change costume, at the director's discretion. Otherwise, everything they need is on the coatstand.

Colin Crowther

MUSIC COPYRIGHT

A licence from PHONOGRAPHIC PERFORMANCES LTD, 1 Upper James Street, London W1R 3HG is needed whenever commercial music recordings are used.

ACKNOWLEDGEMENTS

The extract from *He Wishes for the Cloths of Heaven* by W.B.Yeats is included with the kind permission of A.P.Watt Ltd on behalf of Anne and Michael B. Yeats

To
Mary

TRYST

An open stage with three main acting areas: DR, C *and* DL

The area DR *represents, by turns, an art classroom in the local college, where Jan teaches a weekly evening class, and her studio, which is simply an unpretentious room in her home. Both are represented on stage by a large easel, beside which, at the opening of the play, is a blank canvas. (Behind that are other canvases, showing completed paintings). There is a high stool with a built-in footrest and a small trolley on castors with all her painting materials*

The area from C *to* UC *represents first an art gallery and then the living-room of Brenda's and Tom's suburban semi. It consists of a long, low well-padded bench, of the sort provided in municipal art galleries for the comfort of visitors, but which can also, perhaps with the addition of a couple of cushions, be an acceptable sofa. Beside it stands a low round object, which is unremarked in the art gallery scene, perhaps because it looks like a round litter-bin, but which, when the lid is taken off and upturned, is transformed into a side table for the sofa. When upturned, it has a cloth cover. Inside this box are Brenda's knitting and Tom's magazine. To the* R *of this acting area is a modern coatstand with a dressing gown, apron, cardigan and walking-stick. If facilities allow, this central acting area could be raised on a dais to provide more visual interest and to make the living-room more convincing*

DL *are two chairs, facing each other but slightly separated. These chairs represent a hospital consulting-room and a room in the local vicarage. There would normally be a table or desk between the chairs but this is not visible. (Brenda and Tom use only the US chair: the person they are addressing is assumed to use the downstage chair, but is never seen)*

Before the play begins, music plays: Saint-Saëns, "The Swan", from Carnival of the Animals, *arranged for piano. The stage is in darkness*

The Lights come up. Brenda is UC, staring off L. She is in the art gallery, carrying her handbag, trying to distract herself by looking at the paintings

Tom is DL, in a hospital waiting-room (an empty space), trying to distract himself by looking very closely at a painting on the wall off L

Jan is DR in her classroom at the local college, waiting for her weekly evening art group to settle down. She speaks over her shoulder to the audience, who are assumed to be her class

Jan (*a little nervously*) Just take a seat. Oh, anywhere. With you in a minute. Right. Welcome. Where to start? Painting. That's what we're here for. Art. (*She gets into her stride now*) It appeals to everyone.

Brenda That's nice.

Tom What's that supposed to be?

Jan Why? Because it cuts through words and thoughts and gets straight to the heart. And in art, that first impression is the hook.

Brenda God I wish he'd hurry up!

Tom What's keeping him?

Brenda walks on down the invisible wall of paintings from UC to L. Tom paces the waiting-room, nervously

Jan That first impression catches your attention. It hooks you. Then the artist draws you in — to see something else — pulls you deeper, closer, changing what you see, think, feel. Changing you.

Brenda (*going back to her original picture*) The light. In all that darkness, glinting off a cold grey sea.

Tom (*looking at his picture*) Tangled, frightening, nightmare images.

Brenda A thin ray of hope.

Tom But somehow — coming together — making a strange sort of sense.

Brenda I could live with that.

Tom Perhaps one day I'll wake up from this nightmare and think ——

Brenda It *will* come right.

Tom It *will* make sense.

Brenda In the end.

Tom and Brenda freeze

Jan So that's the job of the artist. Not to paint a picture so much as to share how that — person, place, object — how it makes you feel. To say: this is Tom, Brenda, whoever. This is what they look like, how they behave — but look again, look deeper. This is the sort of person they really are, this is how they make me feel — about them, about myself. That's how art changes you: it creates one impression, draws you in, draws in the person you think you are — then you see another layer, a different image. *And that change changes you.* All art does that, can do that. (*Dismissively*) Except photography.

Tom and Brenda come out of their reveries. Tom is being addressed by a nurse in the hospital, Brenda by an attendant in the art gallery (both of whom do not appear)

Tom Sorry?

Brenda No. No, I'm fine. Thank you.

Tom Must have been talking to myself.

Brenda Thinking aloud.

Tom Sorry.

Brenda Fine.

Jan Photography merely records a fact. Art comments on that fact, interprets it, gives it meaning. It doesn't just say, "Oh yes, that day at Margate. Do you remember, dear?" Been there. Done that. What's the point! No. Art takes you back and makes you experience again how it felt — when — I don't know — that wave suddenly broke over the sea wall, drenching you to the skin. You felt powerless, frail — suddenly, terrifyingly mortal. Now do you remember?

Brenda (*allowing herself to be led to the bench*) Thank you. I didn't mean to ... I don't usually ... But it was raining so hard ... Is that the time?

Tom What? Oh. About time.

Tom follows the nurse into the consultant's room, DL. *He sits in the* US *chair and faces the consultant, whom we cannot see, but who clearly occupies the* DS *chair, a desk (invisible) between them*

Jan Thus one impression, one relationship, builds on another, as each layer of paint builds up, till you and I, creator and spectator, are bound closer, closer than powder and egg white in paint. *We are the paint and we are what is being painted.*

Tom Good-morning, doctor.

Brenda Perhaps I will, just for a moment. If I'm not in the way. I am a little —— (*She sits, looking round the gallery, enjoying the rest of the paintings*)

Jan Oh, I know. This is only an art class at evening school. We're just here for pleasure. But to get any real pleasure out of art — any art — book, painting, play — you have to ... It's like life — you have to plunge in, headlong, heart first, into another world and dare to open your eyes, and believe it, then cling on to that breathtaking, heart-wrenching, life-changing vision while you fight back up to the surface, and it is only the surface, this here, this now ... Risk it. Risk everything for it. (*She shrugs*) For some of you — most of you — coming back to school will feel like going back to childhood. Well, that's as good a starting-point as any.

Tom I'll try. Difficult, though. To relax, I mean. (*To himself*) It's a bit like entering the headmaster's study, coming to a hospital, seeing a specialist, specially one who's seen inside you.

Brenda I used to paint. As a child. And a teenager. But I gave it up. The way you do. Grow up, give up. That's life. I haven't been inside this gallery — any gallery — since I came on a school trip when I was eleven. Hasn't changed. Still feels like a museum or ——

Tom A dentist's waiting-room.

Brenda A mausoleum. (*A short pause*) Gives you the shivers.

Tom Give me the creeps — hospitals.

Brenda Art galleries.

Tom Me? Oh, fine, fine.

Brenda I wish he'd let me go in with him. If only to the waiting-room. At least then I'd know ——

Tom Oh, she's fine.

Brenda Typical man. Didn't want any fuss. As if it's *us* that make the fuss!

Tom No. Not this time. Gone shopping. Better that way. Keeps her mind busy, stops her fretting.

Brenda But oh, no, he had to go it alone. As usual. Leaving me outside, worrying, as usual. Fretting what he'll say: what he'll remember to tell them, what he'll forget to tell me.

Tom Just about the same, really.

Brenda (*suddenly aware the attendant is speaking to her*) I'm fine. Really. Fine. (*She looks around for something to say, some way of proving her sanity. She indicates the gallery*) It hasn't changed. Not in thirty years. Same old red walls. But at least the pictures are different. ... Yes? ... Oh. Nice.

Jan So how does the artist get below that surface impression? With these? (*She indicates her trolley*) Paper, pigment, pen? No. (*Demonstrating*) With this. And this. With hand and eye. And heart. That's how you make someone stop and say ——

Brenda That's nice. That's very — nice ... horrible word, but you know what I mean. The sort of picture you can't take your eyes off. Like seeing someone for the first time — a total stranger — and knowing they are going to be part of your life forever. Like Tom. Soon as I saw him, I knew. I thought, "Oh, so that's the one".

A sort of surprised recognition. Unlike Tom. Took him nearly three years to know his own mind, his own heart. But I knew. I just waited. Sometimes I think that's what my life's been about, waiting. Waiting to grow up. Waiting for Mr Right to come along. Waiting each evening for him to come home from work: coat on the hook, "That you, love?" (as if I don't know); meal on the table, "Had a good day?" (as if I don't know); sit on the sofa, watching telly, me knitting, him reading; waiting for him to notice. "How was your day? Meal was nice. You look tired. Had your hair done?" I could wait all night … And I do. I sit looking down into the fire — he prefers central heating but I need a real fire, real flames, something to get my hands dirty with, something to make for myself, I can't explain, not to him. I wait for the flames to die down and the real fire to glow, that strong, deep glow, that's when it's best — like a marriage, when the passion's burnt itself out and you're left with a good warming glow that you look at and think, "That'll last, that will, this long, cold winter through. You've worked hard to build that, now sit back and enjoy it". I try to show him, to make him see, and once, maybe twice, he's nodded and said, "That's nice … very nice".

Jan First you must get your eye in. The eye of a child, of a child's imagination. Look up. What do you see? Literally, what is there before your eyes? Look down. Draw it. Don't go back, don't correct, don't apologize, just draw what you see. Any pad, any paper will do. For a pencil, something soft, say 4B. But sketch. Catch it, now, quickly, before it moves, before the light changes, the moment passes. First impressions!

Brenda I'm just Her Indoors. Waiting. While he goes off and does the living. For both of us. (I hope, for both of us). I'm so ——

Tom (*rising, in pain; impatiently*) — sick of waiting! Tired of being put off! No more prodding, no more probing, no more tests, no more X-rays, no more samples and charts and tubes and bloody sharp needles!

Brenda (*sensing something and rising*) Tom!

Jan Look up. What do you see?

Tom Now. Tell me now!

Jan Look down. Draw it before ——

Brenda Of course, it's all changed now. (*She walks aimlessly* DR *a little*) His illness saw to that.

Jan No repetition, hesitation, deviation, or you'll miss it, miss the moment ——

Tom Just tell me the truth. Now! As you see it — now!

Brenda (*looking desperately about her*) "Change and decay in all around I see".

Tom Is that so hard?

Brenda (*partly to herself, partly to the attendant*) He had a heart attack.

Tom (*to his consultant*) I know that.

Brenda Two weeks later ——

Tom I know what happened.

Brenda His heart stopped. Cardiac arrest.

Tom I've seen death, felt it, faced it.

Brenda A week after that ——

Tom That was then.

Brenda They carried out an emergency heart bypass. Four grafts. No, five.

Tom Five. I know. And it didn't work. Still I get the pain.

Brenda We kept telling them.

Tom Even now, if I walk to the shops I have to sit down. If I walk back I have to lie down. Can't get — enough — breath — enough … Still pain, here … No energy, strength, stamina. We kept telling you. No-one ——

Brenda Finally ——

Tom Finally you did that scan.

Brenda Two strokes he'd had.

Tom I seem to stop … Suddenly run out of steam … My brain — slows. Like a long faint. This arm goes … Leg … Lose … Can't talk … Find words.

Brenda And almost daily now, more, tiny strokes. Transient ischaemic attacks, they call them.

Tom (*sitting, breathless*) I'm all right. Just let me — (*Pause. He recovers*) I need to know. What *now*? What *next*?

Jan The light has changed. They've moved on. What d'you see now? Look up.

Brenda (*looking more closely at a painting in front of her*) That's so beautiful.

Tom (*still breathing hard*) In your waiting-room. There's a painting. Won't go away. Like a nightmare. Keeps coming back.

Brenda Grey sea reaching out to green island, caught in a shaft of pale sunlight. How I wish I'd seen that, instead, in my dreams, every night, I see, keep on seeing ... When his heart stopped ——

Tom I saw — I keep seeing — my body grinding to a halt, like an old record player running down. Heart: thump, hurt, thump, silence. Feeling: alone but not lonely, more — cut off. Not like someone had turned off the lights, turned down the sound — more like I couldn't make the connection any more, make the link that turned pictures into places, words into voices. Disconnected. That's how you feel when you're dying – there, but not getting through. Like that picture.

Brenda I still see his face, one minute normal, the next suddenly red, then pale ... I called the ambulance — and watched him turn white, then grey ... I could hear the ambulance ringing — quite grey — knocking at the door — I came back and he was blue, lips quite blue, hands so cold, face clammy. I could see him — fading, fading away.

Tom There but only faintly there. Still me, still aware, but fading.

Brenda Ambulance. "Stand aside, love. Leave it to us." Losing contact. Hospital. "Just wait in here, dear. The doctors are with him now." Losing sight of him. "We're taking him up to Intensive Care now, Brenda" — do I know you? — "We don't really encourage visitors up here". What gives you the right to call me *Brenda, love, dear*? I want to be with him. Hold him. "All right, but just for a minute" — as if I'm some spoilt child. And what had they done that I couldn't? Undressed him. Put him to bed. I could have done that. I needed to do something — to reach out, touch him, feel ... . Can't they see that? "There, there". I'm no better. When I finally got in, all I did was pat his hand. "There, there." Then it was, "We think you'd better go home now. Nothing more you can do here. He's in safe hands" — but not my hands! — "We've got your number. If there's any news, we'll let you know". Royal "we" to little "me". (*She shakes her head*) I don't want to go. Not home, without him. (*She builds to hysteria during the following*) Sitting, waiting, by a phone, waiting for a voice I don't know to tell me what I don't want to know! I don't want any more news!

Tom (*calm now, but steadily firm*) I don't want any more tests.

Brenda (*calming down during the following*) Any more drama.

Tom Any more delay. I just want ——

Brenda Life to go on as before.

Tom — to take back control of my own body ——

Brenda A different kind of waiting.

Tom — of my life.

Brenda To draw the curtains against the wind and rain and see just him and me in the glow of a fire that will last this long, cold winter through.

Tom I want my life. What's left of it.

Brenda My husband. What's left of him.

Tom Home.

Brenda Together.

Tom Now.

They are both calm now

Jan (*clapping her hands together suddenly*) Caught. Like a butterfly. (*She opens her hands slowly*) There it is. In black and white, flesh and blood. Ask yourself: how does it make you feel?

Brenda Numb.

Tom Tired, that's all. You know.

Brenda I know.

Jan There you have it. Your subject and how you feel about it. Now: what else do you need to know?

Tom (*with great care and precision, summoning all his energy and concentration to get this right*) Two heart attacks, two strokes, open-heart surgery. And still I can't ... I need to make arrangements, to know how much time I've got left so we can ——

Brenda Treasure it.

Tom Enjoy it.
Brenda ⎱ (*together*) Together.
Tom ⎰

Tom listens while his consultant speaks to him. Occasionally, Tom nods. Brenda waits. There is a long pause

Jan And that's it. The key, the essence. You have your sketch, your first and true impression. Now you have to share it. Through colour, line, shape, from life on to canvas, from three dimensions to two so it can become four: make it artificial, make it art to give it a new, more intense reality that will speak, not just to you — but to any passer-by.

Brenda (*absently*) "Tread softly because you tread on my dreams".

Jan And you start — (*she leans over and picks up the blank canvas and places it on the easel*) — with this. A blank canvas. This is the easy part!

Brenda (*brightening up*) I'm suddenly hungry, terribly hungry. (*She roots round in her bag, takes out a sweet and starts chewing it*)

Jan (*demonstrating to her class*) First, prime it. Use this, it's like emulsion. Just slosh it on. All over. Then while you're waiting for it to dry, take another look at your sketch. You're looking this time for the right angle. Turn it, this way and that. Try and see it afresh, from a different angle, to see what happens next.

Tom (*rising*) Thank you. It can't have been easy for you, but I am grateful. And I am … fine. Good-morning, Doctor.

Tom turns and walks out of the surgery, up and round in a great meandering sweep from DL to UR, heading for the gallery. He is outside now. He slowly realizes this and begins to take in his surroundings: the street, the traffic, passers-by, the gallery. He pauses. He is breathing with difficulty, his chest is hurting, but he is calm now, determined, at peace

Inside the gallery, Brenda, still looking at her favourite picture, backs her way to the bench and sits down

Brenda I could live with that.

Tom I can live with this.

Jan Replay the scene in your mind. Fast forward. Rewind. Pause. Find the moment. Freeze it.

Tom enters the gallery. He reaches in his overcoat pocket for his angina spray and uses it. He comes up behind Brenda, fighting to regain his breath. Brenda feels Tom's closeness, but does not look away from her painting

Tom puts a hand on Brenda's shoulder. Her hand closes on his hand. Pause

Tom Time to go home.

Jan And there you have it. The moment, and the secret of that moment, pure — essence!

Tom Ready?

Brenda In a minute. Look at it, Tom. Isn't it … ?

Tom (*looking, puzzled, at the row of paintings on the "wall" to his* L) Yes. What's the red dot for?

Brenda (*only looking at her painting*). What?

Tom On most of these — a red dot in the corner.

Brenda It's an exhibition — work by local artists.

Tom School of Red Dot, are they?

Brenda It means they're sold.

Tom But this is a Municipal Gallery. They can't sell stuff like that! It belongs to … (*but he can't find the word*)

Brenda You can here. They're local artists. A temporary … Oh, I don't know. The red dot shows which ones have already been sold.

Tom Then why isn't there a red dot on your favourite?

Brenda I don't know. Maybe no-one likes it.

Tom You do.

Brenda Yes, but I like you.

Tom Always said you had funny taste.

They embrace

Brenda Individual.
Tom Highly.

They kiss

Brenda Home?
Tom Home.
Brenda What did they say?
Tom (*simply*) Time to go home.

Brenda looks at Tom closely for a moment, then heads for the exit
UR, *fumbling in her bag for her car keys*

Brenda I'll get the car. Bring it round to the front.

Brenda exits UR

Tom watches Brenda go, then calls over the attendant

Tom Excuse me. That painting. Is it still for sale?
Jan And that's it, really. Paint it, frame it, sell it. Anyone can teach
you that — pure technique. But to use your eye, your heart, that
has to come from you. No-one can teach you that. So, choose your
angle: portrait, landscape. Your medium: oil, watercolours, acrylic
— they're popular with beginners — pastels, my favourite.
Whatever suits, really. And just get on with it. When it's done,
slap it in a frame, put it in a local exhibition and hope you can land
some soul you've hooked. Someone who now sees your vision as
their own, so vital a part of their new, changed life that they will
say ——
Tom (*doubtfully*) How much?

A classroom bell rings in the distance

Jan hears the bell and looks up suddenly. She checks her watch

Damn. Time's up. Same time, next week?

A sense of rush. Jan removes the painting, moves her stool and the trolley into different positions, then reaches for her painting coat and puts it on. From this we glean she has come home to her own studio and it is, at least, the following day. (During the following scene she angles her easel US *so we cannot see what she is painting as she gets on with her own work)*

Simultaneously with the above, Tom steps forward, as if into the street. He looks up. It is raining. He turns up his coat collar, hides the (invisible) picture under his coat, smiles to himself, waves to his wife and steps forward to open the car door

All the above distracts our attention from Brenda, who enters the UC *area*

Brenda takes off her coat and perhaps puts on her apron. She crosses to the bench, upturns the bin, making it into a side table, takes out her knitting and Tom's magazine, then settles down on the sofa, occasionally looking up from her knitting to the picture, now hanging over her mantelpiece, (which is imagined to be DC*), then down to the fire she has made in the grate below it*

Tom enters UC

Tom takes off his coat and hangs it up on the rack. He comes forward, looking at the painting proudly

Tom Well?
Brenda It's lovely. I can't believe — how much?
Tom (*putting on his cardigan*) You're worth it.
Brenda Ah!
Tom Just. (*He begins to wheeze and pant and has trouble with the cardigan*)
Brenda Let me help you.
Tom I can manage! (*He sits heavily, quite exhausted, picks up his magazine and pretends to read*)

Brenda stands watching Tom, then crosses to look into the fire. There is a pause while Tom gets his breath back

Brenda How long?
Tom Mm?
Brenda You know. (*She sits on the floor and gently pokes the fire*)
Tom (*putting down his magazine*) Any day, any week.
Brenda (*quietly, frightened*) God!
Tom We knew ——
Brenda Yes, but not ——
Tom Up to a year. If we're lucky.
Brenda Lucky!
Tom (*rising and taking a few blind steps* L) It could happen fast. Another heart attack. Or slow. Another stroke.
Brenda (*turning and kneeling and looking up at Tom*) Oh my poor love!
Tom (*turning away from Brenda, not wanting her to see him cry*) I've got the easy bit. Just lie down and ...

Brenda comes up behind Tom and holds him

It's you I feel sorry for.
Brenda Why?
Tom You've got to go on.

Brenda's face is desolate as she surveys the barren wasteland of her future

Brenda Oh I'll be fine.
Tom (*turning suddenly*) I hope not!
Brenda (*holding Tom's face in her hands*) You know what I mean. Cup of tea?

Tom shakes his head

No more tests?

Tom (*returning to the sofa*) No.

Brenda Good. Strange. I feel better now.

Tom Me too.

Brenda I suppose we ought to be sad. Start crying. Or something.

Tom I don't think I've any tears left.

Brenda (*kicking a coal back on to the fire*) No, I cried my heart out, at first. Now? I'm tired of weeping. I still cry, but it's like when we make love, my mind keeps wandering off.

Tom Wandering … ?

Brenda Oh yes, you know. I go sob, sob, and notice the lampshade's got a cobweb.

Tom When you say ——

Brenda I can't seem to help it, these days, I just go with the feeling.

Tom I'll remember that.

Brenda (*smiling*) No you won't. (*She moves* US, *round his side of the sofa*) Admit it, you do the same.

Tom Well, sometimes, I mean, I can't help it, sometimes I imagine it's not you but ...

Brenda I feel lighter somehow.

Tom Yes.

Brenda (*leaning over and kissing Tom on the top of the head*) I suppose, because we know.

Tom (*flapping Brenda away, like swatting a nuisance fly*) Hate that. I'm not frightened any more.

Brenda There's nothing more to be frightened of. We know the worst. We've faced it before. We know it can't hurt us, can't separate us. We can face it, out-face it, together.

Tom I feel like a drink. (*He picks up his magazine*)

Brenda (*sitting, as it were, on the back of the sofa*) So do I.

Tom Your turn.

Brenda What do you mean — you imagine it's not me?

Tom Never mind that — what about the bloody cobwebs?

They do a double-take, then dissolve into laughter and a hug. Tom shudders, then goes limp. He is having a transient ischaemic attack, which has all the symptoms he described earlier to the consultant. Brenda tenses. Is this the end? She lowers Tom's head on to her lap

Tom (*weakly, with difficulty*) I — love you — so much.
Brenda Together, Tom, always together.

Tom falls asleep. She strokes his hair

He's mine now. All mine. But how many times can you say good-bye? (*She rises*)

Tom sleeps on

He has these attacks — what? Once? Twice a week? Sometimes twice a day. Any one could be the last. And he's changing. The illness, I suppose. He used to be a man with an illness. Now he's an illness, wrapped up in a man. He's becoming more dependent, more like a child. And what does that make me? That's what I find so exhausting. Not what's happening to him, but having to play all these goddam parts! Am I his lover, his wife, friend, nurse — or his bloody mother? (*Pause*) I pray God he goes quickly. A heart attack, not another stroke. Please, God! A child I can cope with, but a baby … !

Tom (*in his sleep*) Brenda?
Brenda (*sitting beside him*) At least — at last — he needs me. (*She hums her child a lullaby*)

Time passes

The doorbell rings

Tom hears the bell and wakes

Jan, a paint brush in her mouth, a rag in her hand, reacts to the bell

Jan Damn!

Tom struggles to stand and take off his cardigan

The doorbell rings again, more insistently this time

Jan Right with you!
Tom I must go.
Brenda (*rising*) I'll take you.
Tom No. I must go on my own.
Brenda But where?
Tom Something I must ——
Brenda You're not well enough!
Tom I'm not dead yet!

Brenda sits, as if she has been hit. Tom gets his coat and a walking stick

Tom (*feeling guilty*) I promised.
Brenda Who?
Tom Secret.
Brenda I won't come in with you. You can have your little — tryst ——
Tom Nice word.
Brenda — but let me at least drive you there. I'll worry sick.
Tom I've always wanted to use that word. Tryst.
Brenda Phone. Promise me you'll phone.
Tom I'll be fine.
Brenda Oh, Tom, Tom!
Tom I need to do this — for myself. For you.

The doorbell rings

Jan I'm coming, I'm coming.

Tom turns from Brenda and towards Jan, thereby "entering" Jan's studio. Brenda picks up Tom's cardigan and is left clutching it in great desolation

Jan Yes?
Tom Good heavens.
Jan Sorry?
Tom You're alive. I mean, you really do exist.
Jan Last time I looked, Mr —— ?

Tom Tom.

Jan Oh. Right. Yes. Sorry. I was in the studio. Well, come in.

Tom You were expecting me.

Jan I'd forgotten. Got caught up in ... What do you mean, I'm alive?

Tom It's just that — artists ... I don't know. Somehow one thinks of them all as — dead.

Jan Welcome to my — crypt.

Tom (*looking around*) Oh.

Jan Disappointed?

Tom Oh. No.

Jan No cobwebs or candles. No rats scurrying about.

Tom No.

Pause

Jan I do have a gerbil.

Tom It's just — I pictured a garret, skylight, masses of discarded canvases ...

Jan A rumpled divan. A screen strewn with discarded clothes.

Tom And a feather boa.

Pause

Jan You are sure you came to the right place?

Tom I hope so.

Jan I don't normally see people.

Tom Nor do I.

Jan I mean, at home.

Tom So do I. (*Pause*) Such an ordinary house.

Jan I'm an ordinary person.

Tom You're an artist. You weave spells. Paint dreams. Show us the future in the past. You work magic. Take things — odd, empty things — bring them together, show they belong. You make sense out of all — this. (*He gestures vaguely*)

Jan Sit down, Mr ——

Tom Tom.

Jan Tom.

Tom (*sitting*) I had to come. I was intrigued.

Jan So was I. When the gallery phoned, said ——

Tom They were very discreet.

Jan I gather ——

Tom I don't want my wife to know. A tryst.

Jan I see.

Tom No. You don't.

Pause

Jan Tea? Coffee?

Tom Yes.

Jan (*stumped*) I imagine you want to see my work.

Tom I have seen it.

Jan (*floundering*) People usually ask to see an artist because they like her work. They've bought one piece. They want to buy another.

Tom Do they? I'm afraid I'm not used to this game.

Jan (*firmly, trying to take charge, to impose limits*) It's not a game for me. It's my living.

Tom I do understand.

Jan No. You don't.

Pause

Jan So. Landscape? I do mainly landscape.

Tom And seascape.

Jan Yes. Oh yes. You bought ——

Tom *View to the Isle of Skye*.

Jan I remember.

Tom It meant so much to my wife.

Jan (*putting canvases on to the easel, to display them to him one by one*) This?

Tom (*acutely embarrassed*) Oh, yes. Very ...

Jan Or this.

Tom Erm ...

Jan This.

Tom Lovely.

Jan But not quite ——

Tom I've just come from my solicitor. It's hard to explain. I had to make a will, you see. I thought it was a Last Will and Testament, but apparently that's died out — the Testament. Nowadays all anyone's interested in is the will: not the meaning, just the money. The will's fine; just a matter of disposing of what you've accumulated. Like a tree shedding leaves for the winter. I'm getting used to that. But a Testament, surely that still matters — matters more — even if no one's there to read it: what your life adds up to, what you've learnt, that has to matter — or what price life?

Jan Fascinating.

Tom Well it would be if I could remember any of it. Trouble is I had a stroke. Two.

Jan I — don't know what to say.

Tom (*looking at her closely, then nodding*) Yes, it is hard to find the words. (*Small pause*) Strokes play games — with your memory — like hide and seek. Only they cheat — stealing the words you want, the thing you want to do, and hiding it where you can't find it, and when you go looking for — whatever — they take away your memory of — it — so you know you're looking but you can't remember what the hell for. And the frustration builds. To rage, blind, white rage. (*Pause*) I think I've gone off the point.

Jan Words.

Tom They were — there — like pebbles in a pool. I could see them. All I had to do was plunge in my hand and pick just the one I wanted, hold it glistening up to the light — play with it, build with it. Now I can't even see — them. The water — so muddy. I stick in my hand and feel and grab. I hold it to the light. Just sand. A handful of sand! (*He lapses into a confused silence*)

Jan waits, then tries to help Tom

Jan And you want me … ?

Tom I can't put — into words — what my life has meant to me. So I thought: could you draw me a picture?

Jan Of — your life?

Tom Yes. Sorry. Tired now. Only bits of energy now. Fits. Fits and starts. Then — then I start winding down — like an old — thingy — record thingy. (*He loses focus and sits staring blankly, still responding when spoken to, but not really with us, during the following*)

Jan (*concerned*) That's a very tall order.

Tom Not really. If it has a meaning it should be easy to find, surely?

Jan But hard to express. Who is it for, this Testament?

Tom My wife, Brenda.

Jan Brenda.

Tom (*reviving slowly and standing up*) I'm dying. I want to leave her something.

Back in the living-room, Brenda, still desperately alone, reaches out for comfort. During Tom's following speech she smells the cardigan and cuddles it

Something that will say, "Thank you. Thanks to your love I'm a different person now. Growing … " (*He loses track again. He moves to the studio window and looks out* DL) Growing up, I remember, I used to stare into the mirror, hate what I saw — think, "How could anyone love that?" I was so full of hate, self-doubt, fear, I became — prickly.

Jan (*quietly reaching for her sketchpad*) Like a hedgehog.

Tom Yes. Pushing people away. I knew no-one could possibly love me, so I set out to make myself — unlovable, I suppose, to prove I was right all along.

Jan We all do it.

Tom (*to himself*) Stupid, stupid. (*Answering Jan*) We do? Fancy. A nation of … hedgehogs. (*He laughs, then goes vacant again*)

Jan A world. (*She sketches him during the following*) Go on.

Tom I was at a party, I think it was a party … Suddenly, I felt someone looking at me, looking through me. Tried to shrug it off.

Wouldn't let go. I looked up and saw her, saw Brenda, and thought, "No matter what I do, those eyes will never leave me, the look in those eyes will follow me to the end of my days." I tried to get away, to hide, for months, years, but those eyes, the feeling they knew me — understood — accepted me — that feeling just kept growing.

Jan So you pushed her away.

Tom I didn't want to hurt her, couldn't bear the thought of disappointing her.

Brenda puts Tom's cardigan round her shoulders and is comforted

Jan (*prompting Tom*) But her eyes?

Tom Said, I'll take that risk.

Jan's pencil snaps

Jan Pass me another pencil, will you?

Tom moves to the trolley, roots out another pencil and passes it to Jan

Tom So we got married and slowly, slowly, I began to grow. It sounds corny ——

Jan (*shrugging*) Everyone's love story sounds corny to someone else. Doesn't mean ——

Tom (*defiantly*) I felt like a plant when the sun comes out. I started to ——

Jan Plant? What sort?

Tom Strange. I saw a plant once. When I was on retreat. I saw this ... Nice little thing it was — blue flower, tiny leaf — and I thought, "That's me." Don't know why. Did then. Forgotten now.

Jan (*looking at her sketch*) Damn!

Tom What?

Jan Rubber.

Tom (*passing Jan a rubber*) I looked it up, when I got back. I'm a keen gardener, lots of books on it. Flora and fauna.

Jan And it was?

Tom Ragwort.

Jan What?

Tom Common in hedgerows and ditches.

Jan How — nice.

Tom I'd hoped for more than "nice".

Jan Sorry.

Tom I thought I was more special than "nice", than just a common ragwort. Silly, I know. But what you go through everyone goes through. It's how you react, how it makes you feel, that's unique, that makes you special to you.

Jan I've been trying to tell my students that.

Tom You can't tell it. Words are not … (*He struggles for the word, miming "sharp"*)

Jan (*guessing*) Sharp enough?

Tom nods

I don't know. Some words.

Tom looks doubtful

(*Searching for an example; then*) "Yea though I walk through the valley of the shadow —— "

Tom No. "*In* the shadow".

Jan " — I shall fear no evil."

Tom Why should you?

Jan Well — death — doesn't everyone?

Tom But shadow means shelter. We need that shelter like … Like my ragwort needs the hedgerow. The shadow — the valley — is where we belong. (*Pause*) I learnt that. From Brenda.

Pause. This is all beyond Jan. She searches for a way to politely decline his commission

Jan Tom ——

Tom I am loved, so I belong. And in the shelter of that love, I grow, I become what I was — who I was — meant to become.

Jan suddenly grasps Tom's meaning and at the same time sees something she can draw

Jan Don't move.
Tom No. Don't draw me. That's not what I want.
Jan But surely ——
Tom Draw the meaning, but leave me out of it. (*The exertion is too much. He can't breathe. He uses his angina spray. Pause*) I'm sorry. This isn't … I've wasted your — time … So precious … time. (*He turns* us, *to leave the studio*)
Jan Tom?

Tom turns in the doorway

Come back.

Tom shakes his head

Next week? It will be our — special secret …
Tom (*smiling*) Tryst. The word is tryst.

Tom leaves the studio and during the next speech returns home, hangs up his coat and goes to sit by his wife. After a pause, and without looking at each other, they simply and quietly hold hands

Jan I tried. First a portrait. That was easy, obvious, but the eyes, I couldn't get that look. Then him sitting in a chair looking out through open windows, curtain flapping in a summer breeze, view down onto a shore, sea, sky, blue sky. Paradise. But that little crumpled figure seemed so lost, so broken, like a dried leaf. I was afraid the wind would blow him away. (*She shakes her head and discards the sketch*) I tried again.

The doorbell rings

Tom I must go.
Brenda Again?

Tom rises and moves to the coat rack. Brenda follows him

Is it not something I can do for you — with you?

Tom shakes his head, too tired to talk. He puts on his jacket this time and takes his stick. He heads DC

(*Calling after Tom, angrily*) Is it worth it?
Tom (*with difficulty*) Has ... to ... be.

Tom walks DC, *leaning more heavily on his stick than before, his breath hurting. He looks down into the river — where the audience is — and then ahead, to the opposite bank. He seems to draw comfort and calm from this*

Perhaps at this point we hear a little of the theme music: Saint-Saëns, "The Swan", played this time on the cello

Brenda looks in Tom's cardigan pocket and finds his angina spray

Brenda Tom! You forgot ...

But it is useless. He is far away. Brenda looks in the other pocket and finds a piece of paper

Brenda (*reading; pronouncing it "Yan"*) Jan? Who's Jan? Oh, Tom.

It is the last straw. Bewildered, angry, hurt, Brenda rushes DR, *but before she has gone many steps, she seems to hit a brick wall.* (*This, and the following, are mimed*) *She looks up; she has found the great porch door of the local church. She touches it, feels for the handle, tries to turn it — but it won't budge. She tries harder, kicks the door, then hammers on it with her fists*

Open this door! You promised! Oh —— (*She falls to her knees, despairing*)

A shaft of light illuminates Brenda, as if the door has been opened

I thought … it was … locked.

The music stops. Brenda stares up at the face (invisible to us) before her

During Jan's next speech, Tom turns US, walks slowly into the artist's studio and sits on the high stool

Jan I tried again. This time I left the chair empty, his stick leaning on it, a mug of coffee half-empty, still warm, on the window-sill, a book open beside it, a Bible perhaps. You'd have to imagine it open at "Where your heart is …". Whatever. As though he'd just stepped out through the french windows, footprints in the sand, leading into the sea, basking in the sun, floating up into the sky. (*She looks at the picture, sighs, and rejects it*) Why does someone else's meaning seem so corny? Start again.

During the following, Tom's voice is clear at first, but he soon tires and gradually begins to slur some of his words

Tom Christmas — always meant a lot to Brenda. And to me. Presents under the tree, candles, church. Hope born anew. This Christmas, I won't be here to share that with her. I don't want her to feel — hopeless. I want to give her — leave her — something — special.

Jan A portrait.

Tom (*tiring*) No. No looking back.

Jan Landscape.

Tom (*slurring*) Look forward.

Jan Seascape.

Tom (*despairing*) Perhaps.

Jan Abstract.

Tom (*frustrated at himself*) No. Real.

Jan (*sarcastically*) A real painting of the view ahead?

Tom (*with innocent hope in his face*) Yes, that's it.

Seeing Tom's look, Jan just sighs and fetches out her sketchpad

Jan Let's try again.

Brenda moves to the vicarage, DL. She grasps the back of the chair and sways while she talks to the vicar's wife, who is seated opposite her

Brenda I'm so sorry. I don't know what you must think of me. I don't know why I came, really — I just needed someone to rail at, someone bigger than me. So I went to the church but the door was … When you opened it, I … Thank you. Just for a moment. (*She sits*) I'm sorry to bother you, I didn't know your husband would be out. Better, really. I've had enough of men for one … Coffee? Thank you. No sugar. Got to watch my … (*She looks down at herself*). Who am I kidding? What the hell — two. Two sugars. (*Shouting*) And a biscuit. Sorry. I mean, if you have one.

It is clear the vicar's wife has gone into the kitchen. Sure she is alone, Brenda goes on

It's like a tap — that garden one — always sticking. You want to turn it off but … I thought, "He's got nothing now, no-one to distract him. No more work to make him feel useful, no more meetings to make him feel important, no more parties to make him feel successful." Felt quite glad about that, if I'm honest, though when he was first ill, I was grateful for any distraction myself. Cards, phone calls, visits. People are very kind. They just can't seem to keep it up … He's been ill too long — outlived their concern — now it's turned nasty, they hold back, "give you space". And I was grateful for that too, at first. Just him and me now. We can face it. Together … Now I see … I'm … not enough. He's all I want, all I need. But I'm obviously not everything he wants. It's the same when people call. He's just sitting there, gazing off into space. The doorbell goes and he perks up. When they leave, he slumps back. I only ever seem to get that slump.

Brenda mimes the vicar's wife returning and handing her a mug of coffee and a biscuit

Thanks. Nice. Oh, Bourbon. My favourite. (*She nibbles. She drinks*) It's like he's shedding an old skin. Something he doesn't need any more. Letting go. (*She drinks*) Oh, I'm no better. I do it too. But not the same way. When someone is ill — like he is ill — and you know that any minute he could ... You start to grieve — I don't know, for what might have been, all sorts of daft things — and the trouble is, with grieving, you can't stop it. Like that damn tap. It sounds awful but, for months now, I've been trying to get on with my grief, and him being there, well, sometimes, oh it sounds awful, but sometimes he gets in the way. Can you understand that? Forgive that? I can't. No wonder he's found someone else. This Jan. (*She eats, hungrily*) I'm really enjoying this. Thank you. Ages since I had a ... Once, on top of the wardrobe, I found this magazine. Well, two of them, actually. I wasn't prying, just tidying. Same way I found this. (*She holds out the piece of paper*) I thought, "Well, if he'd asked, I could have done that, worn one of those. Why does he need some dirty tart to do it for money when I'd do it for free? For love?" (*She rises suddenly and "spills her coffee"*) Bloody men! Bloody, bloody men! Oh damn, I've spilt on your ... . That's the trouble, isn't it? They make a mess, we clear it up. If we make a mess — who's to clear up after us? (*She "hands back her mug"*) Here. You'd better have this back before I do any more damage. And I'd better get back to my — leaky tap. That's the trouble. You can turn it on, but you can't turn it off, can you? But you'd know all about that, being a vicar's wife. Thanks for — and the Bourbon. My favourite.

Brenda turns US *and effectively exits from the vicarage. She freezes*

The Lights DL *slowly fade to black-out*

Tom And what have I got to show for it? I'm forty-six — (*insert the actor's real age*) — not much in the way of savings — I hope it's enough to pay the funeral costs.

Jan You had your work?

Tom They replaced me as soon as they heard.

Jan That must have hurt.

Tom Relief, really.

Jan Life must go on.

Tom That's what hurts. (*Pause*). So, wealth, work — nothing there, no lasting memorial there. (*He rises*) All I have is Brenda. All we have is each other. And that — is that — enough — to justify — life ... my — life? (*He moves to the studio window*) On my way here, I stopped in the park, looked down into the river. On the opposite bank — two trees, roots in the water, branches lifted up to the sky, trunks wrapped round each other, growing into — through — each other, reaching up toward the light. Like looking in a mirror. Somehow ... (*He pauses. Then he begins to root in his pockets for his angina spray*) I must go. I seem to have left my ——

Jan Come again. One more — what did you call it? One more tryst — I think now that's all I'll need. Just one more. (*Inspired, she draws, almost frantically, during the following*)

Tom and Brenda enter their living-room at the same moment, but from different sides of the stage. They look at each other with new eyes

Brenda All right?

Tom Fine.

Brenda You forgot your spray.

Tom Sorry.

Brenda I'll get your tea.

Tom hangs up his coat

Jan (*reaching for the blank canvas*) Base dry? Right. Start to transfer your sketch on to the canvas. I like this bit.

Tom Sit down.

Brenda It's time for your tablets.

Tom There's something I want you to do for me.

Jan Set out your palette.

Brenda Will you be going out again?

Tom No.

*Brenda relaxes. The rest of the scene is light, warm, tender but not
at all mawkish*

Jan Draw in the horizon. Two-thirds: one-third. Now start. At the
top. Background. Just stroke it in.

Jan paints through the following scene, but the easel is angled US *so
we do not see what she is painting*

Brenda Well?
Tom I want you to marry again.
Brenda Tom ——
Tom When I die I want you to find someone else. Someone who
will give you all the love, the pleasure, you deserve.
Brenda But Tom ——
Tom Please. I can't bear the thought of you being lonely, alone.
Brenda There's a difference.
Tom Please.
Brenda (*lightly*) All right.

There is a pause. Tom is disconcerted, Brenda smiling

Jan Decide on your source of light.
Tom How — will you … ?
Brenda I could advertise.
Tom No.
Brenda Lots of women do. "Toyboy Wanted."
Tom Brenda!
Brenda "Rich widow seeks even richer widower."
Tom No.
Brenda "Not-rich widow seeks ——
Tom No!
Brenda — older man for fun and friendship."
Tom Certainly not!
Brenda "Old woman seeks geriatric gentleman for a thoroughly
miserable time."
Tom A thoroughly miserable *married* time.
Jan Highlights. Shadows.

Tom Perhaps you could get a pet. Instead. I'm told gerbils are
  quite ——
Brenda Oh, Tom, don't you see?
Tom What?
Jan Main focus now.
Brenda I love you
Tom But I ——
Brenda Now.
Tom But ——
Brenda *You* and *now* are all I have, all I need.
Tom Is that enough?
Brenda It is for me.
Tom (*finally at peace*) And for me.

They embrace. Tom coughs. During the following, Brenda helps
him to sit on the sofa, then gets his dressing gown from the coat-
stand

Jan (*still painting*) At this stage it's always difficult to keep the
  perspective, the balance, so come down to the foreground – to the
  place where you are, now, observing. (*She stops suddenly*) I never
  saw him again. Difficult this bit. Water always is. Trying to keep
  it flowing. I gather, a week later, he had another stroke. A bad one.

The Lights slowly fade on the area UC *during the following*

Tom sits very still, left arm held awkwardly, one foot stuck out
awkwardly, twitching occasionally. With great love and care,
Brenda mimes feeding him yoghurt on a spoon

Brenda I feel — content, now. Not happy, sad, angry. Nothing
  extravagant like that. Full with today: "sufficient unto the day".
  This is enough for me. I am — content.
Jan A month later, he died.

Tom gets up easily, walks round to the back of the sofa and places
his hands on Brenda's shoulders. Then, gazing intently at Brenda,
he walks backwards out of the light

Jan (*as Tom exits*) Finished.

Jan steps back to review her painting. Brenda slowly folds the cardigan

Brenda When it happened it was so casual, so ordinary, I just thought, "Oh". And he was gone. He just sighed … Perhaps that's all that separates life from death: breathing in and breathing out. I never realized it was so simple. That the living and the dead are only ever a breath apart. (*She comes forward and pokes the fire and tries to warm her hands by it*) I'm glad we kept the fire. Something real in an age of pretend. I don't know why people are so afraid to draw close, ashamed to get their hands dirty. There's nothing more satisfying in the world than building a good fire.

Jan (*describing her painting*) On a riverbank, two trees, a willow and an alder, wrapped round each other, roots drinking deep from the same clear river bed, summer leaves sheltering a patch of light-blue ragwort.

Brenda rises, comes DC *and stands looking down as if at a grave*

Jan puts an outdoor coat on and stands, awkwardly, waiting, DR

Brenda The funeral was — mercifully — short. A relief, really. All that waiting — over.

Brenda shakes hands with people as they leave after the funeral. Jan comes up, acutely embarrassed, and hands Brenda a business card. Brenda looks puzzled

Jan I'm Jan. I'm sorry ——
Brenda So am I.

Jan goes back to her studio area and moves things quickly back into position for the art school class. Brenda watches her

Brenda I … waited — what do they call it? — a decent interval.

Jan takes off her coat

Brenda enters her classroom as Jan does this

Jan Just take a seat. With you in a minute.
Brenda Actually, it's you I … When you're free.
Jan (*turning to look at Brenda*) I'm about to start my evening class.
Brenda If you've got a moment.
Brenda } (*together*) Sorry.
Jan }
Jan (*recognizing Brenda*) You're Brenda.
Brenda I wondered if we could ——
Jan (*shaking hands*) It's nice to meet you. Tom talked such a lot about you.
Brenda He never mentioned you.
Jan Well, he wouldn't. He wanted it to be a ——
Brenda Tryst.

Pause. Jan finds she cannot meet Brenda's eyes. Puzzled, she looks away, then sees the painting by the easel

Jan He bought a painting from me. (*She picks it up*)
Brenda (*thinking Jan means the one hanging over the fireplace at home*) I know. It's beautiful. Thank you. The dearest thing I have.
Jan (*startled*) Good. I mean, I'm glad. Look. About Tom. I'm sorry he ——
Brenda I'm not. I miss him. You never stop missing them, but the hurt — like a toothache really — dulls to a sort of aching hole. One of those little aches and pains that remind us we're alive.

Jan stares, the painting in her hands. Brenda barely glances at it

Brenda That's nice.
Jan (*shocked*) Nice?
Brenda I used to paint. Gave it up. Grow up, give up. I think I was wrong. I feel it's time to start again now.
Jan (*trying again to off-load the painting*) He wanted you to have something.

Brenda A Testament.

Jan Yes.

Brenda But you can't just hand someone the meaning of life on a plate.

Jan Well ——

Brenda They wouldn't recognize it. Anyway it might not be true for them. It's something each person has to find for themselves. You're an artist, you'd know all about that.

Jan (*putting down the painting*) Yes. I didn't know him very well.

Brenda Good.

Jan But I do know he wanted me to help you. I think he had this idea somehow, something I could offer, might help soften the blow.

Brenda (*to herself, softly*) I *was* enough!

Jan Sorry? (*She sees her class arrive. To them*) Just take a seat. With you — I'm sorry, I have to ——

Brenda (*much lighter and brighter now*) Actually, you can. Help, I mean. This class of yours. Does it … ? I mean, do you take beginners?

Jan We're all that.

Brenda Could I join? I think I'd like to paint something, about Tom, about me, you know the sort of thing.

Jan A Testament.

Brenda We all have to start somewhere.

Jan Take a seat.

Brenda smiles, happy and relaxed, now. She exits DR

The Lights gradually fade everywhere but DR*, until Jan is lit by a single spotlight*

Jan (*looking at her painting of the trees*) The trouble is knowing when to stop. One dab more. No. Just tidy up those leaves. No, no. You have to learn — and it hurts — to let go. Nothing is ever finished, ever perfect. Perhaps it wasn't meant to be. Perhaps that's how art, all art, in the end communicates, connects, changes people. Through imperfection, incompleteness. Just one impression leading to another. Layer upon layer. Life upon life.

Holding out the promise of another kind of tryst. (*She puts the painting down and places the blank canvas on the easel*)

Music plays under the following, gradually increasing in volume

And you start with this. A blank canvas. This is the easy part! (*She is back in her stride now, riding her favourite hobby-horse, content*)

The music swells

The Lights fade to Black-out

FURNITURE AND PROPERTY LIST

On stage: DR

Large easel. *On* US *end*: painting coat, overcoat
Blank canvas
Canvases with complete paintings
High stool
Small trolley. *In it*: painting materials, including paints and
    paint brushes, rags, pencils, rubber, sketchpad

UC

Long, low, well-padded bench
Cushions
Upturned side table. *On it*: cloth cover. *In it*: knitting,
    gardening magazine
Modern coat-stand. *On it*: walking-stick, dressing gown,
    apron, jacket, cardigan (*In one pocket*: angina spray; *in
    another*: piece of paper)

DL
Two chairs

Personal: **Brenda**: handbag. *In it*: car keys, handkerchief, sweets
Tom: *in overcoat pocket*: angina spray
Jan: watch (worn throughout), business card

LIGHTING PLOT

Property fittings required: nil
Composite set; three acting areas

To open: Darkness

Cue 1	Music. When ready *Bring up full lights on all three acting areas;* *darkness around and between them, if possible*	(Page 2)
Cue 2	**Brenda** falls to her knees, despairing *Bring up shaft of light on* **Brenda**	(Page 25)
Cue 3	**Brenda** freezes *Fade* DL *lights to black-out*	(Page 28)
Cue 4	**Jan:**"A bad one." *Fade* UC *lights slowly*	(Page 31)
Cue 5	**Brenda** exits *Fade all lights except spot* DR *on* **Jan**	(Page 34)
Cue 6	Music swells *Fade to black-out*	(Page 35)

EFFECTS PLOT